In the spring of 2017, when I was asked to collaborate on a book, providing my photographs to compliment the poetry of a friend, something clicked and I decided it was time to refocus my energy on photography. I haven't stopped taking pictures since college when I first started exploring the world through a camera lens. As I revisited my photographic journey, I came across a book of original poems and photographs that I created in the summer of 1977. Inspired by American Photographer, Minor White, I was fascinated by the intersection of photographs and words. There is only 1 copy of the original book, which was made by typing the words onto each Black & White photograph, which I developed myself in the darkroom. I then dry-mounted the pages together and used a spiral binding.

Celebrating more than forty years of exploring the world through photographs and words, I offer this Anniversary Edition to compare them and discover just how far I've come.

Should you wish to see more of my work, please visit my website: www.ThroughSarahsEyes.com
or follow me on Facebook, Twitter and Instagram.

Sarah Routman

Copyright © 2019 Sarah Routman
All rights reserved.
Anniversary Edition
ISBN-13: 978-1975871178

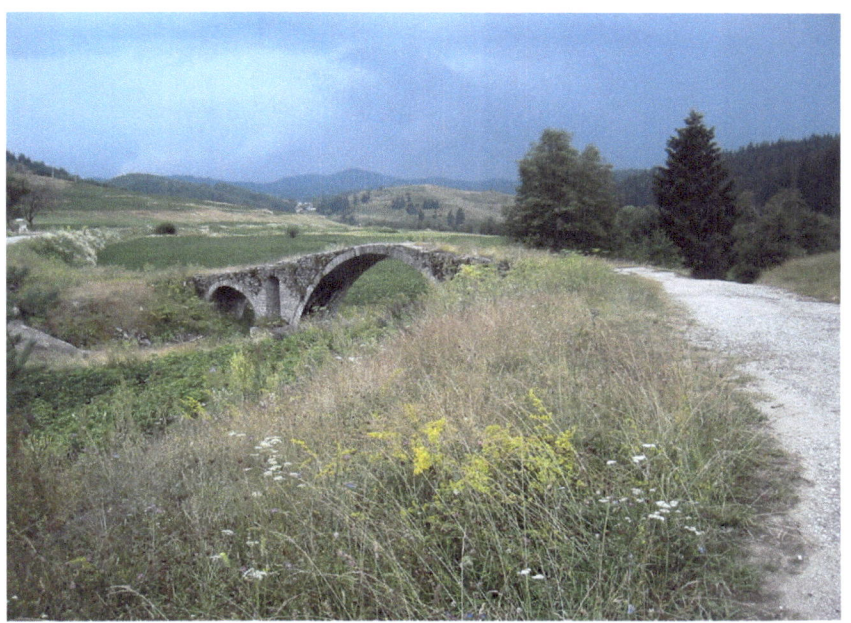

The beauty of life lies in the journey.

Exploring the journey…

I have included a copy of the original book of photographs and poems followed by the new version, which revisits and explores the initial themes. Finally, I offer a juxtaposition of the two.

Light Through Open Windows

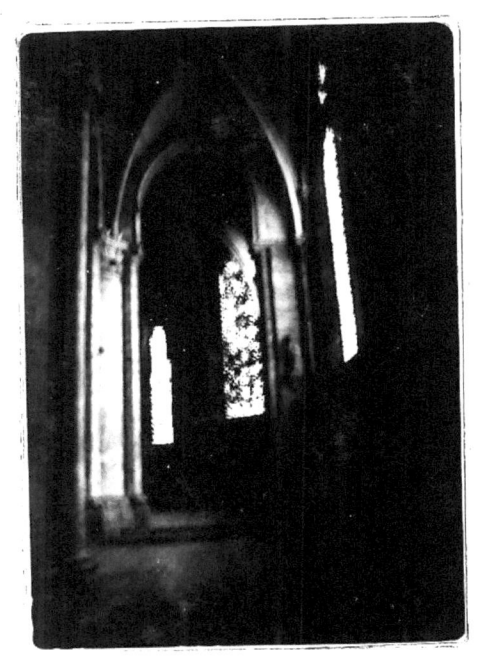

August, 1977
photographs and poems all original
work by Sarah Blum

LIGHT THROUGH OPEN WINDOWS

A true poet
causes you to create many poems
after reading only one of his.
         —Sarah Blum

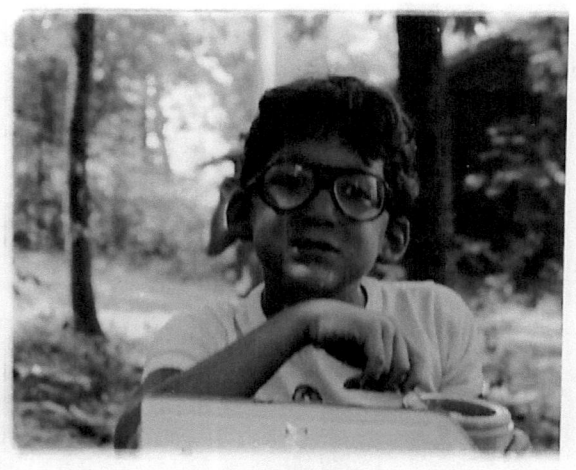

A Child's World

Philosophers, and other fools
sit around the innocent child who drools
at their knowledge, so intense,
that child's fascination ends, and hence
the red balloon he holds escapes the world
and the room forever echoes the words hurled
against eachother or the wall
but it matters little. The child lives it all.

Right away you made me comfortable, as
If to somehow
Catch me off-guard. and
How time managed to slip
Away from us until
   you drank afternoon tea
        in London
  while I breakfasted at home.

   I don't know, or

Remember ever knowing.

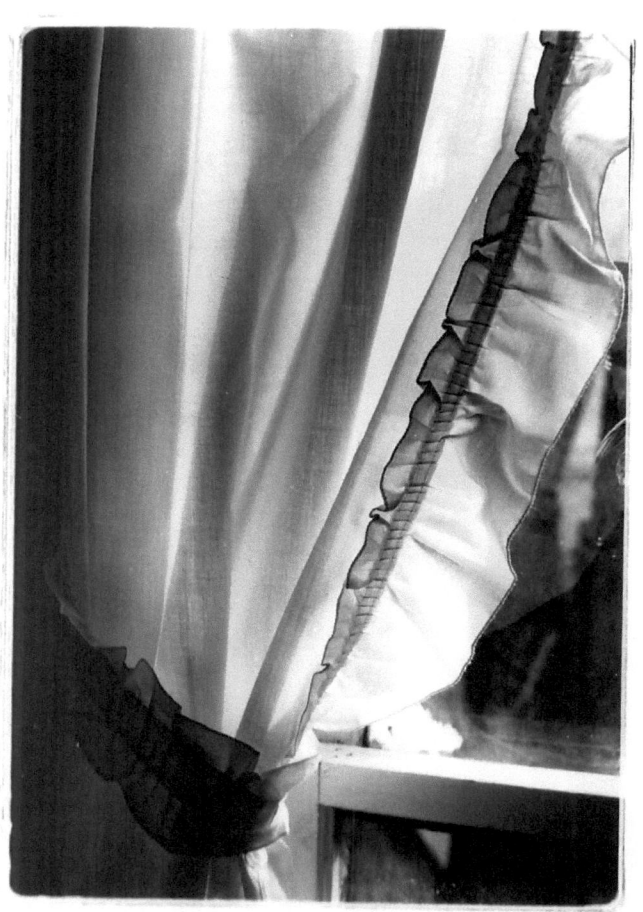

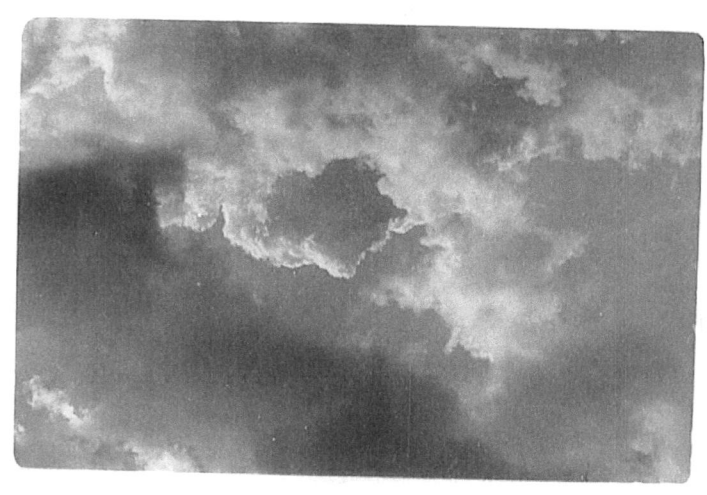

white, little, puffy clouds
  pinches of nothingness –
    leading

                  nowhere...

factories trying to get ahead
      in the world
  forcing thick, gray smoke

             up

     up

 up

    to reach the sky

little innocent nothings
             being
                  weighted
                        down
    and choked until they

    vanish

  into the fresh air,

   leaving a dull, black shadow

     for man to cower under.

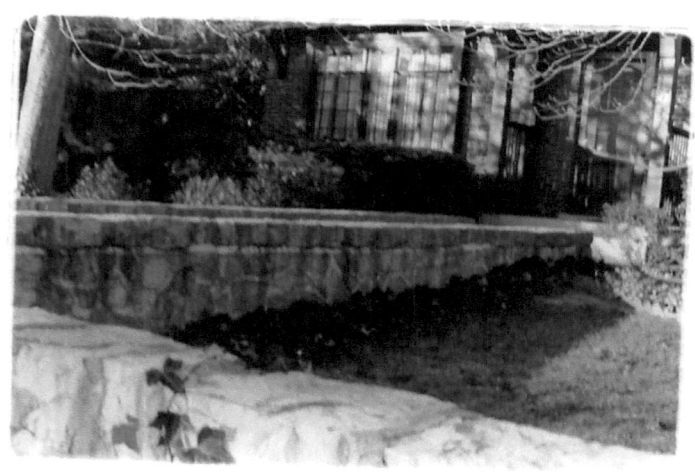

Behind Shadows of the Library Window

somewhere, outstretched
in the gloomy distance
          of the cloudless
     cloudy sky,

you sit, looking out your
          gray window,

thinking, as I am,

   of the distance between us:

of the lonliness in clouds,

  and the beauty of

          an autumn day

peek out among the shadows
    play in the light
   dance with your slender form
the walls will not listen,

    only echo

        ...echo

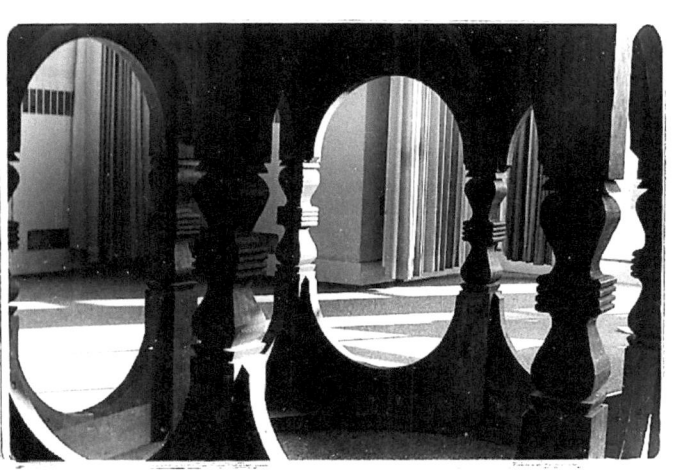

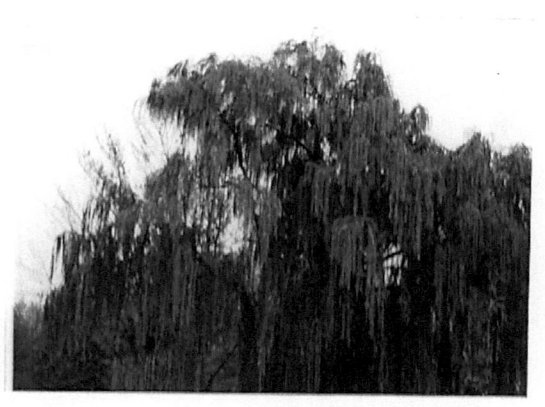

Sojourn at Dusk

So, you can see why I never ventured
 further than my willow tree

for I found contentment there –

 among the swaying branches and
  the evening air
 and the fragrant scents of
  surrounding rose bushes

 and your company

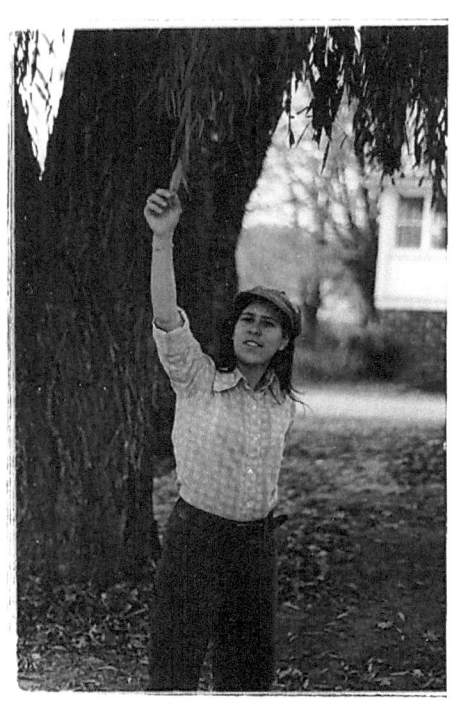

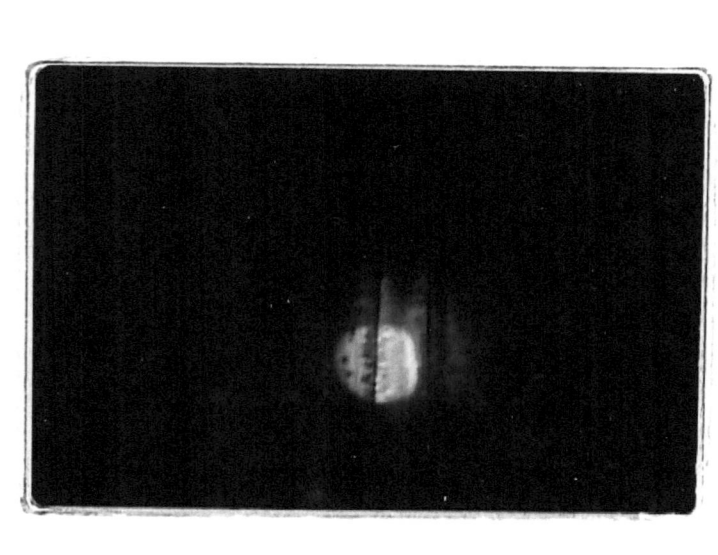

Inspiration Point

when it's dark outside
in the distant time

between morning and night

shadows of our past
cast lights

while time creates images
forgotten by an open window

taking me back
making me remember,
is this light,
reflecting from my window

you can not see
what I find in the shadows
for it is reflections on myself
not light through open windows.

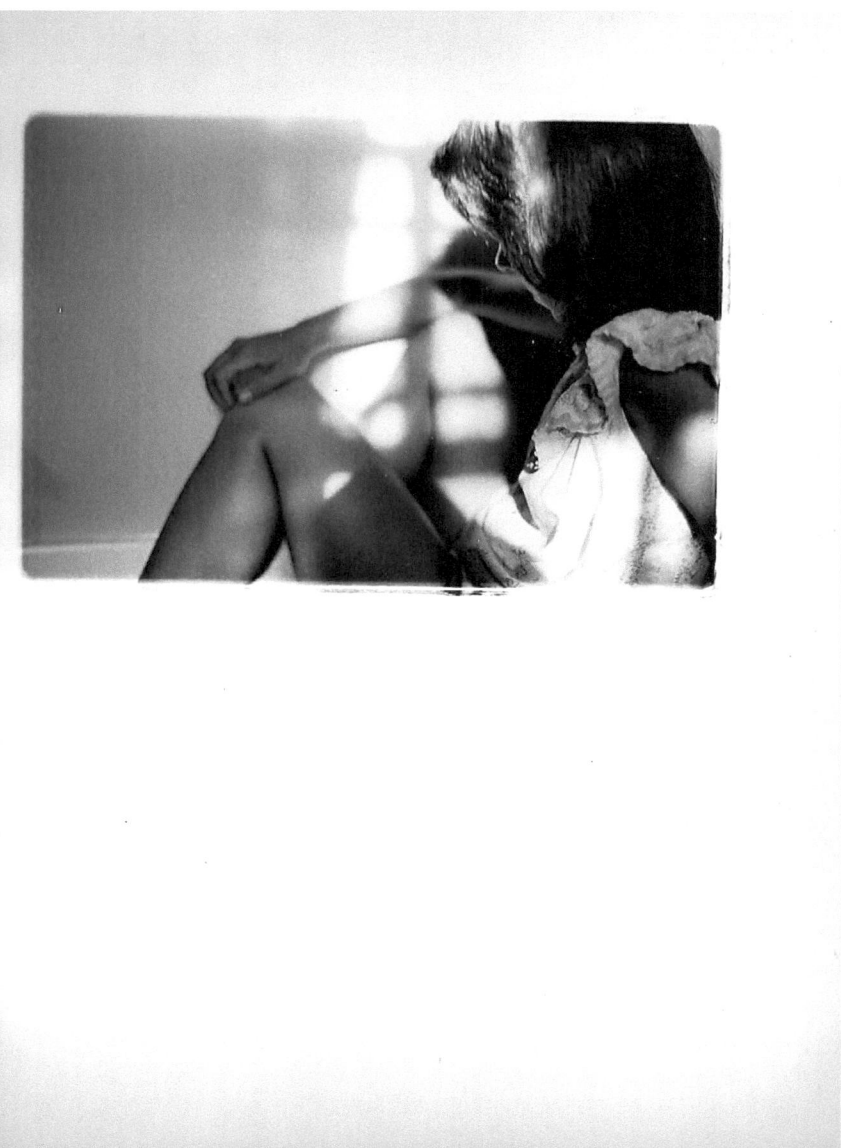

Light Through

Open

Windows

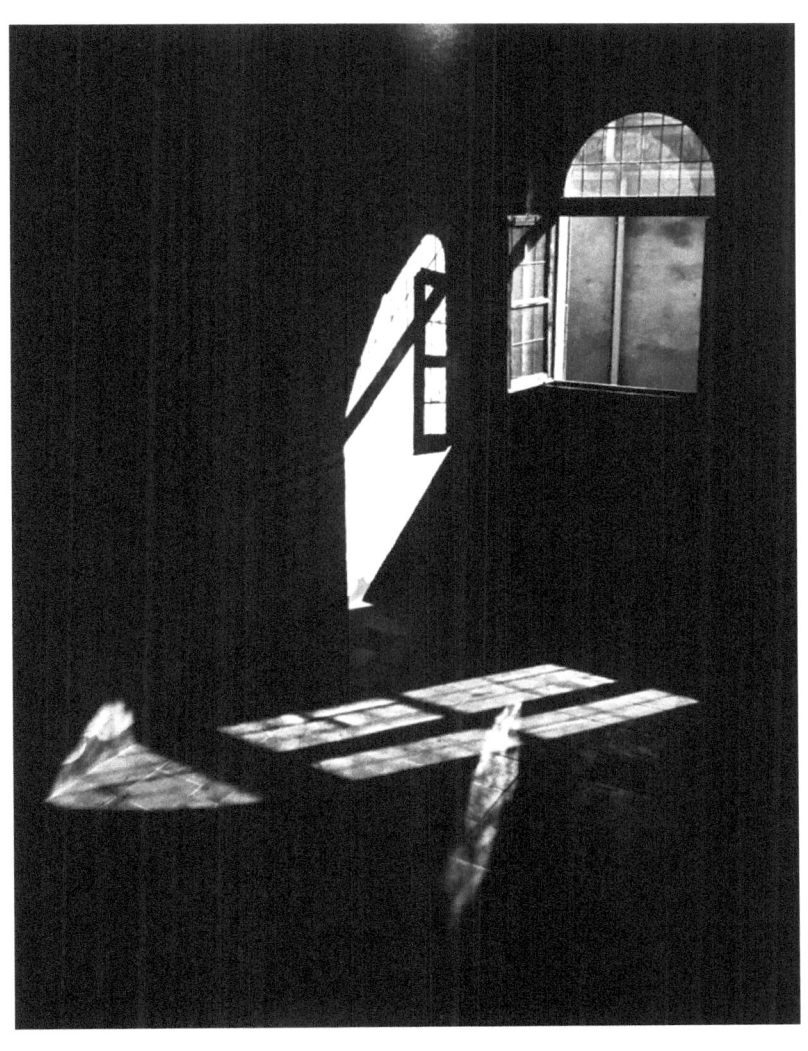

© April, 2019
photographs and poems
all original work by Sarah Routman

Light Through Open Windows

"Poetry is an echo,
 asking a shadow to dance."
          -Carl Sandburg

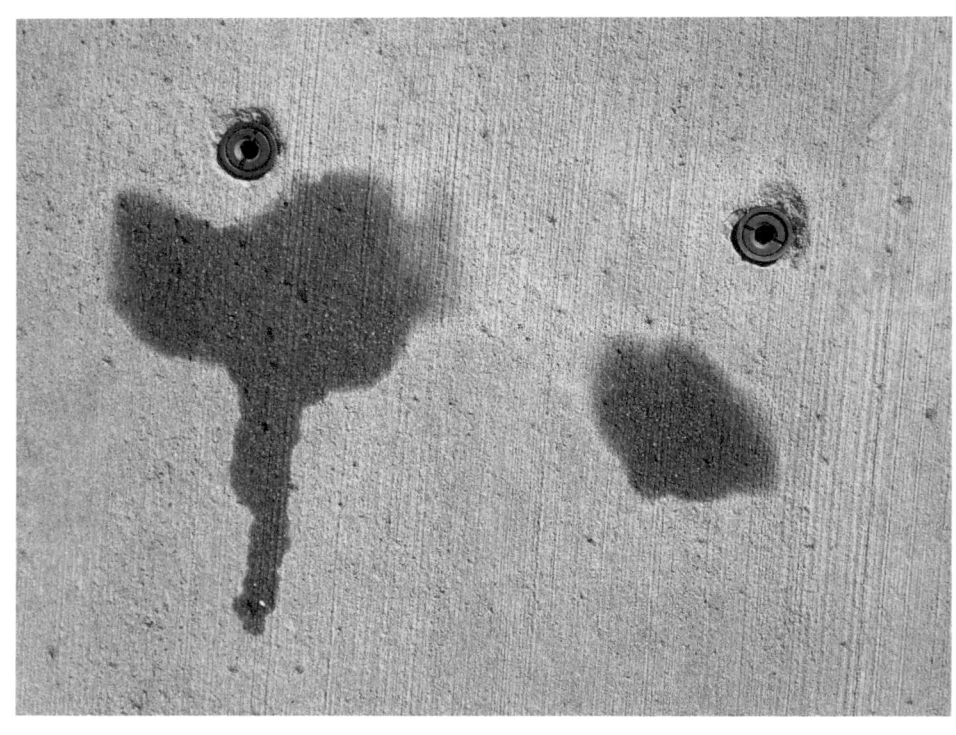

Still a Child

I try to find meaning every day
Make important points with the words I say
I've had numerous jobs, but I'd rather play.
I ask around, try to find my way.
Let harsh judgments sit, wait for them to decay.
I'd give anything to have let love stay.

The world fascinates me still
Is there destiny, fate, or can I exert free will?
The child I was asks so much more, and mourns
The passion so long ago killed.

Miracles travel with me since the day I was born
And still I feel torn –
Is there a G-d? To whom shall I pray?
A younger me passed through the door
And still I muse: is there nothing more?

A quiet breeze caresses the window,
billowing the curtains in the afternoon
of my life.

The scent of hot summer days plays
Tricks on my memories
And freezes time.

I don't know
or remember ever knowing.

Except for the day you told me I did
and then I knew.

And still, I do.

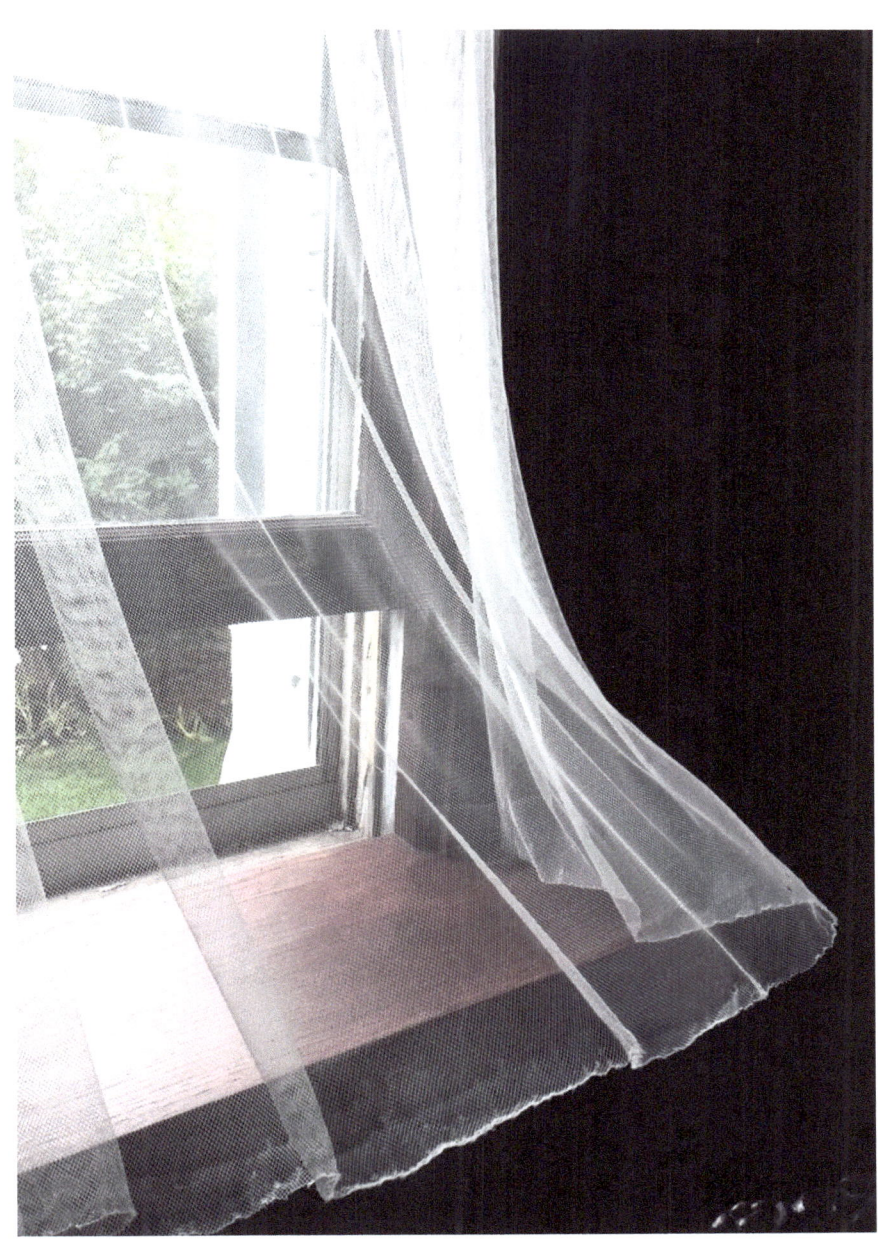

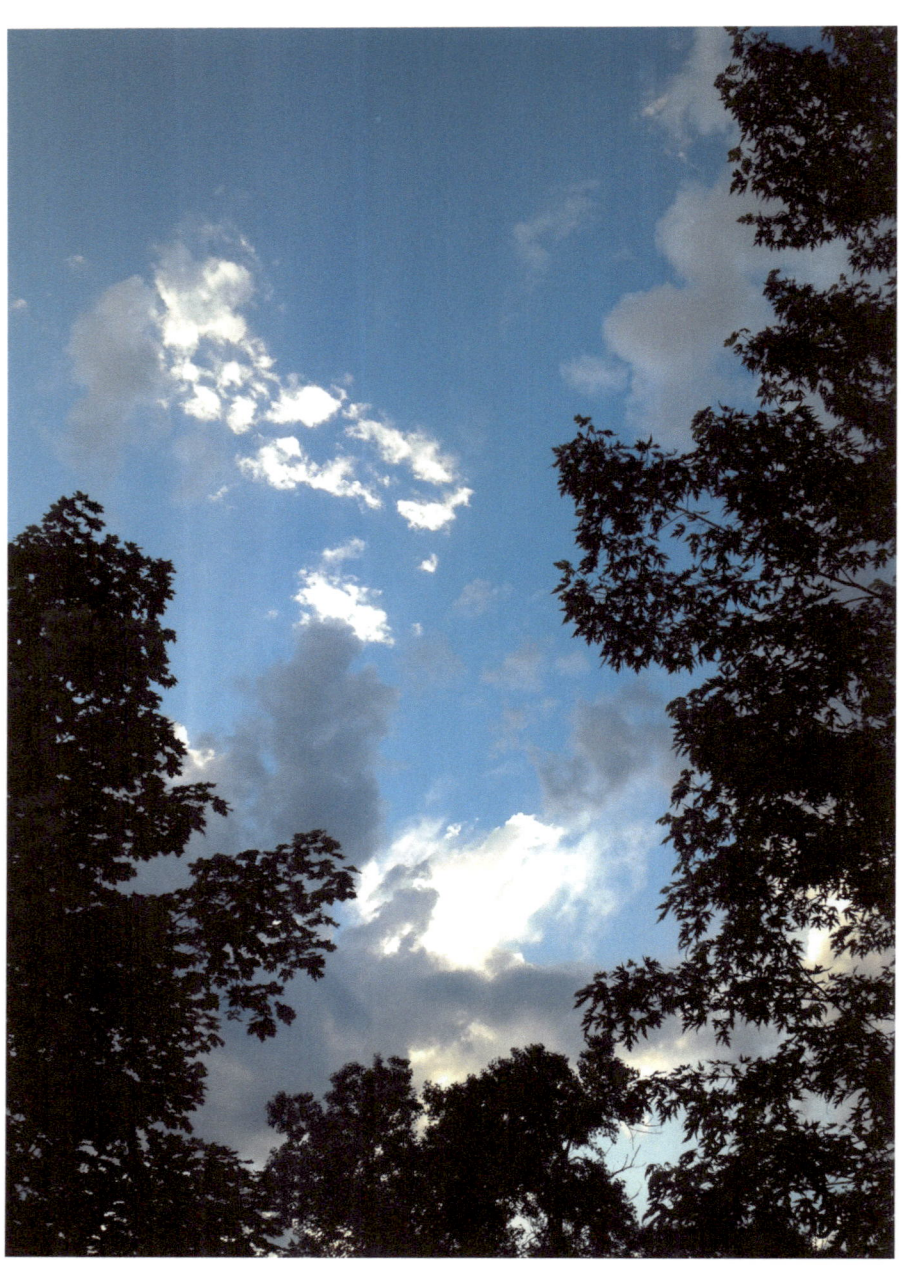

white, little puffy clouds . . .

painting love pictures in the air!
they're everywhere - but I can't
seem to mend the tears

   climate change is very real
BIG BUSINESS continues to lie

                           and steal.

e e cummings has long ago died

now I write poems that try to rhyme

there's a heaviness that sits upon
      my heart

I wonder if I can play my part

the world is cold-no, warmer now

   the clouds turn gray,

     unleash their power
d r
  o p p
     i n
       g
gentle rain in a summer shower.

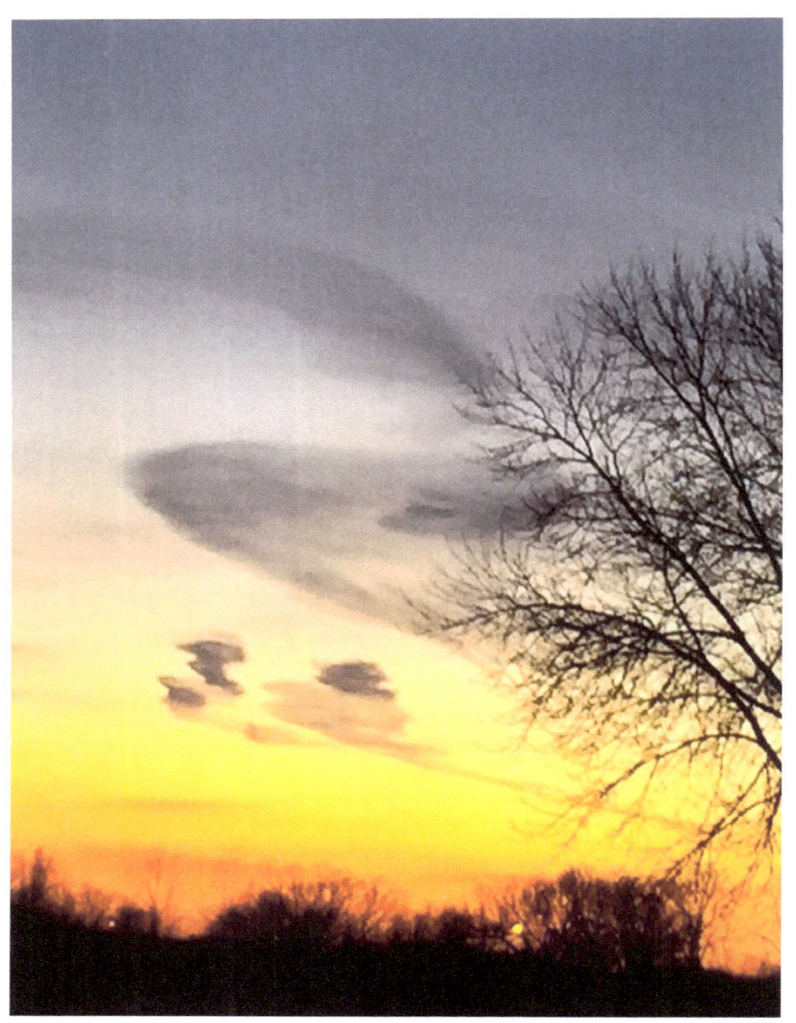

In a Lonely Tree

After many months
of searching,

she found her heart
clung tightly
to an otherwise
naked tree branch.

Hints of red passion
still evident
in the fading sun,

she could still hear
his voice

whisper her name
in the wind.

They will dance
together

In and out
of the shadows

Until the wind
carries them away

Or snow
silences
the music of the dance.

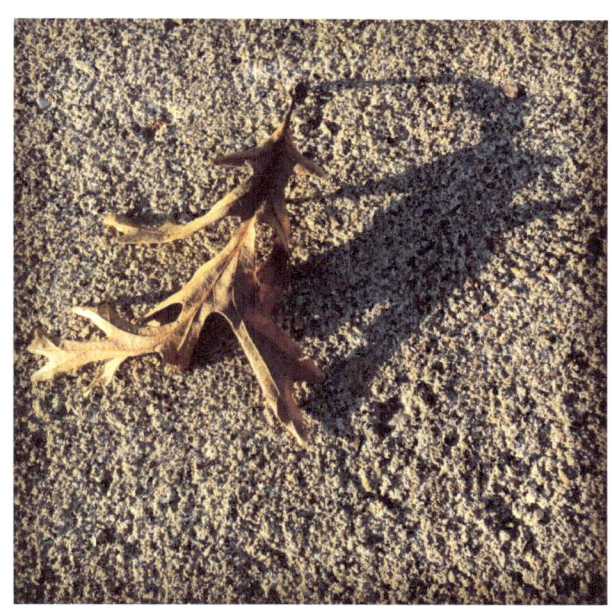

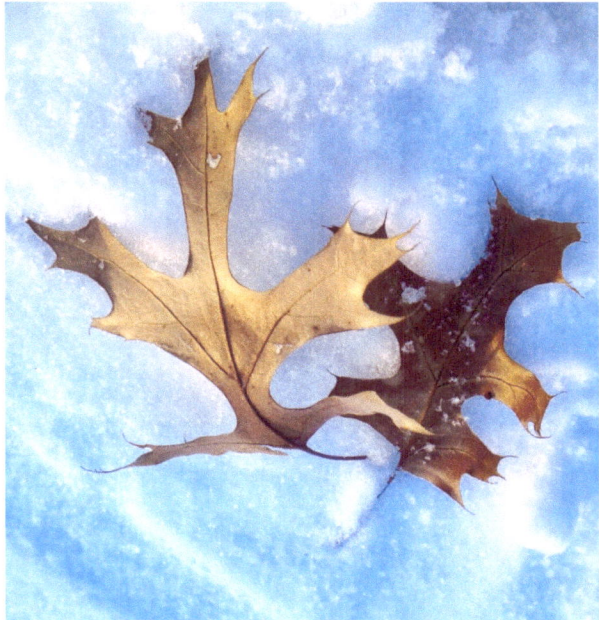

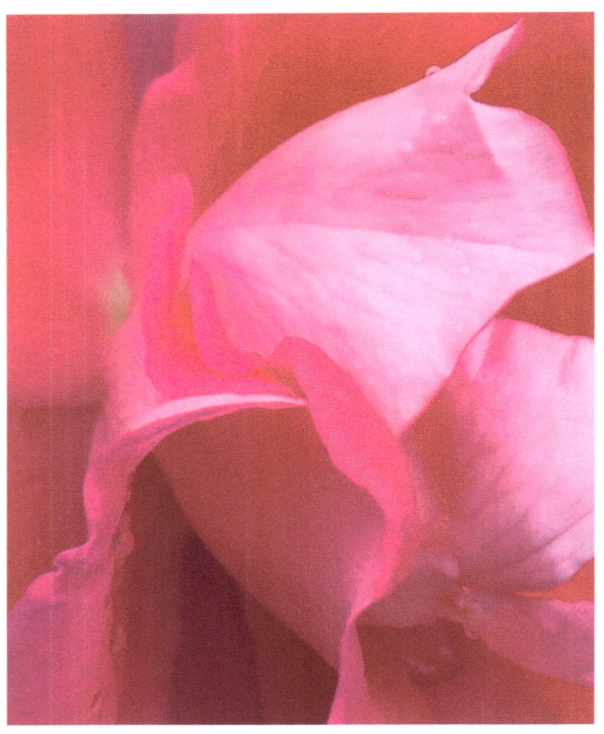

Dewdrops of Softness

In the softness of flower petals
I remember your touch
So I photograph them often,
use them as a crutch
to feel you near me when
the distance between us,
unspoken, becomes far too much.
These tears aren't for all that
might have been,
But for what we *did* have
Those two hours of eternity in the garden.

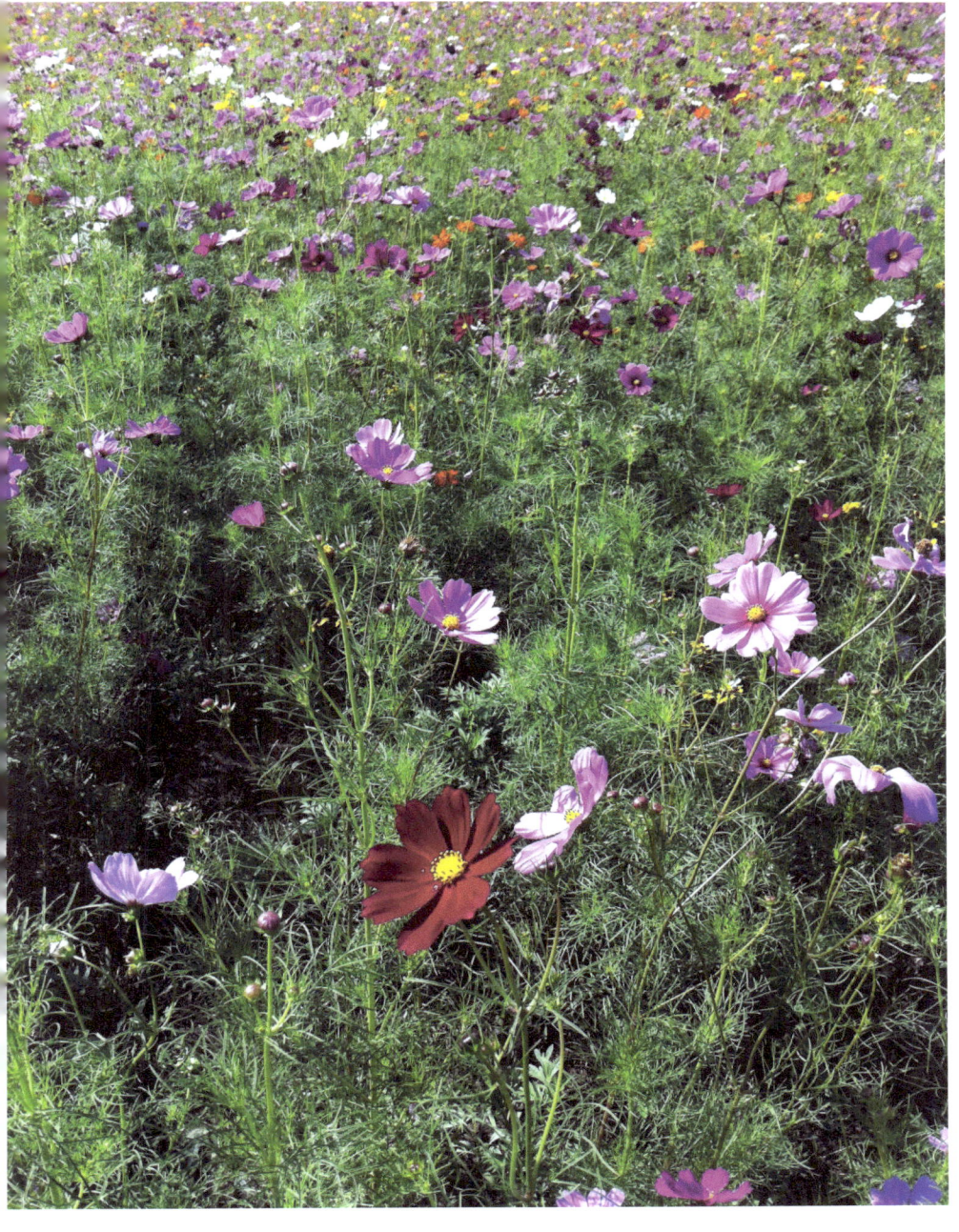

The Same Moon

When I look to the sky
and notice the time

Whether morning, or night
or I manage to rhyme

Your heart beats for mine
Though I may be out of sight

A full moon shines just as bright
Despite living all these years
In two different time zones.

A shadow of my former self -

It's still me,
peering in the window of my soul

Pieces of me scattered,
no longer whole

Ever thinking,

Love rocks in my pockets
sinking

ever deeper into my
romantic fantasies.

Reflections of the past
cast everlasting light

slowly revealed
like light that peeks through open windows.

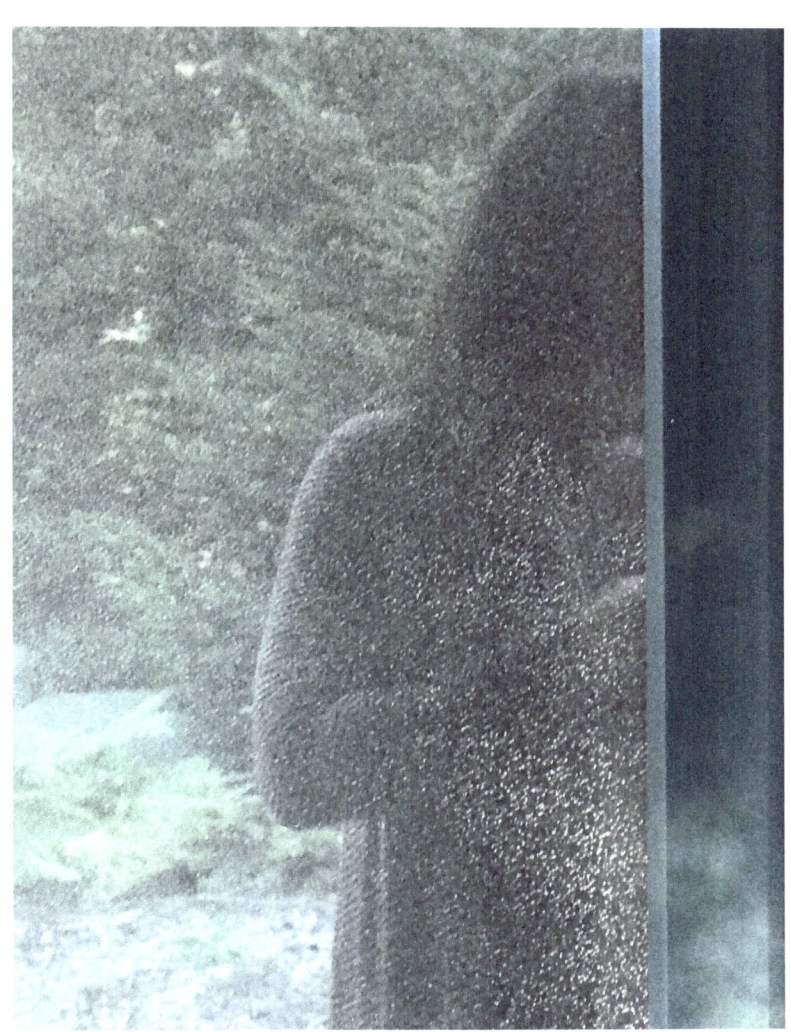

Light Through Open Windows

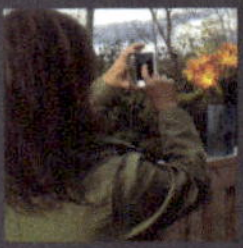

Sarah is a creative person with boundless energy. Finding beauty in places often overlooked by others, Sarah sees the world through her lens of grateful optimism. She believes that attitude can shift everything in life, and makes a point to take walks, take pictures, read books and travel from her home in Minnesota. Sarah brings a genuine love of life to her photography which she began studying in college. In 1977 she wrote, "A true poet causes you to create many poems after reading only one of his." It is her hope that these photographs and poems will inspire your own creative juices to flow. To see more of Sarah's photographs, visit her website: www.ThroughSarahsEyes.com

"When people ask me what equipment I use, I tell them my eyes."
~Anonymous

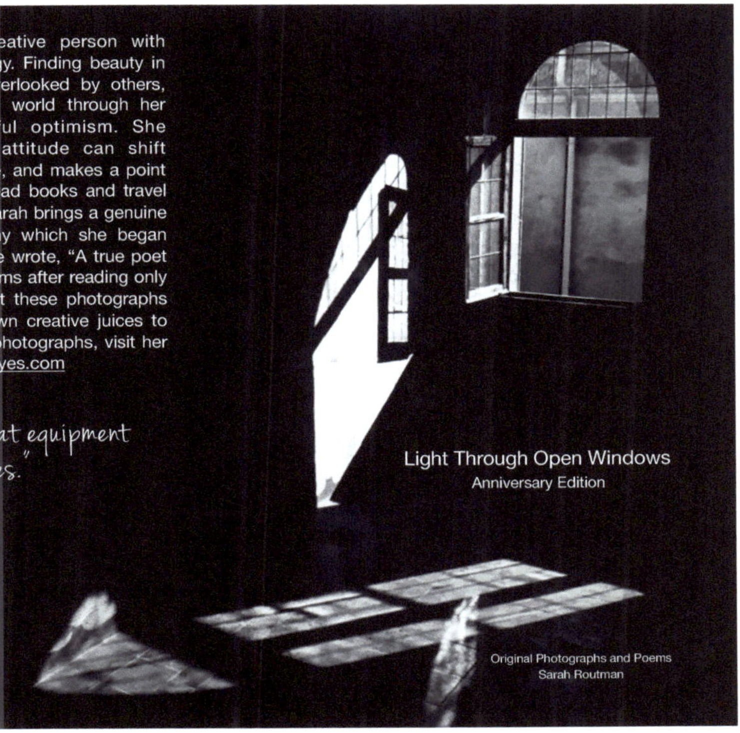

Light Through Open Windows
Anniversary Edition

Original Photographs and Poems
Sarah Routman

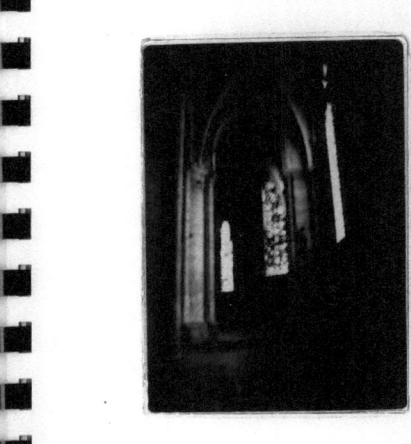

August, 1977
photographs and poems all original
work by Sarah Blum

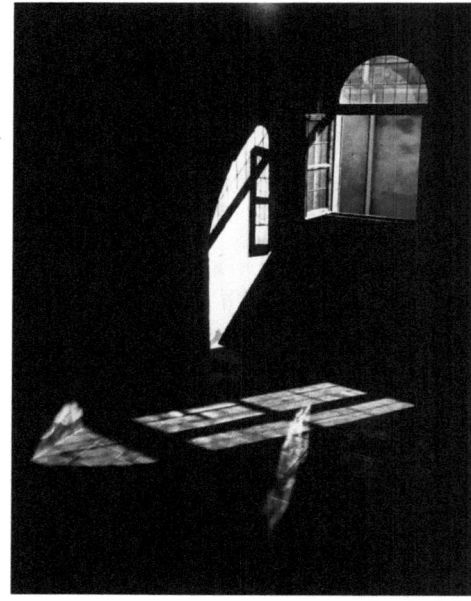

© April, 2019
photographs and poems
all original work by Sarah Routman

LIGHT THROUGH OPEN WINDOWS

A true poet
causes you to create many poems
after reading only one of his.
        -Sarah Blum

Light Through

Open

Windows

"Poetry is an echo,
asking a shadow to dance."
-Carl Sandburg

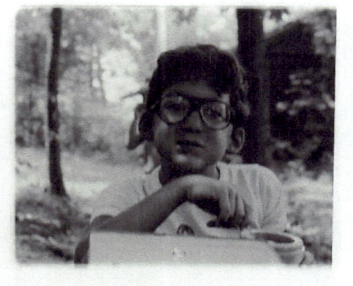

                A Child's World

Philosophers, and other fools
  sit around the innocent child who drools
 at their knowledge, so intense,
  that child's fascination ends, and hence
  the red balloon he holds escapes the world
  and the room forever echoes the words hurled
 against eachother or the wall
  but it matters little. The child lives it all.

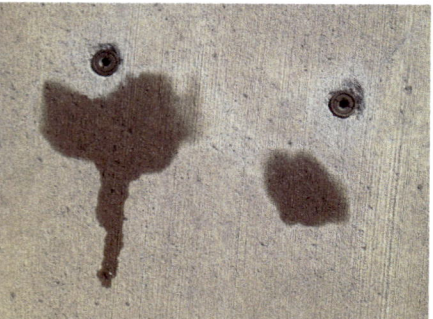

                Still a Child
I try to find meaning every day
Make important points with the words I say
I've had numerous jobs, but I'd rather play.
I ask around, try to find my way.
Let harsh judgments sit, wait for them to decay.
I'd give anything to have let love stay.

The world fascinates me still
Is there destiny, fate, or can I exert free will?
The child I was asks so much more, and mourns
The passion so long ago killed.

Miracles travel with me since the day I was born
And still I feel torn –
Is there a G-d? To whom shall I pray?
A younger me passed through the door
And still I muse: is there nothing more?

```
Right away you made me comfortable, as
If to somehow
Catch me off-guard.   and
How time managed to slip
Away from us until
   you drank afternoon tea
          in London
   while I breakfasted at home.

      I don't know, or

Remember ever knowing.
```

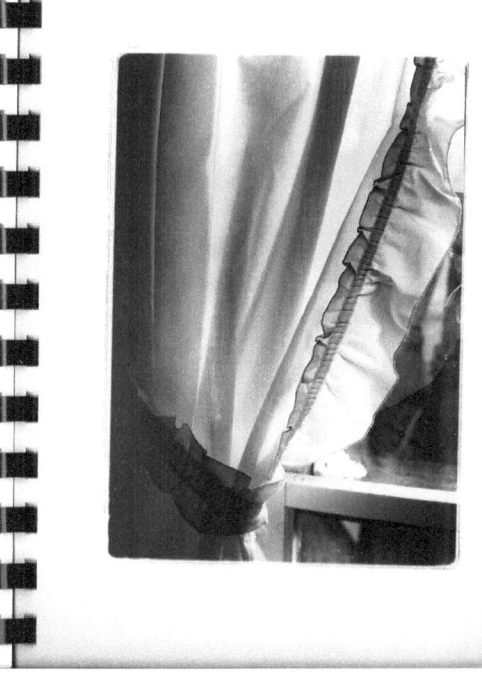

A quiet breeze caresses the window,
billowing the curtains in the afternoon
of my life.

The scent of hot summer days plays
Tricks on my memories
And freezes time.

I don't know
or remember ever knowing.

Except for the day you told me I did
and then I knew.

And still, I do.

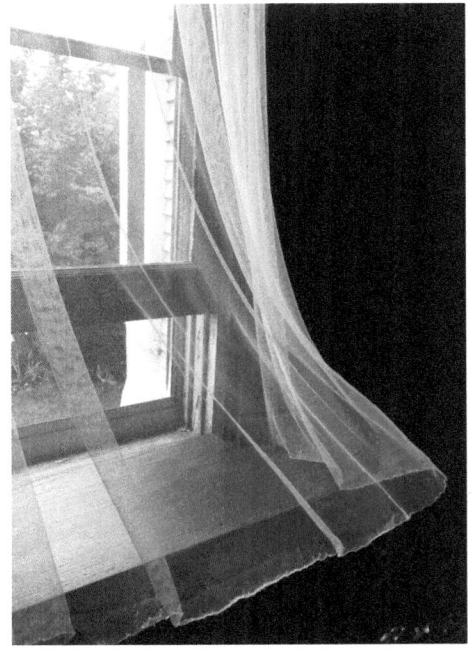

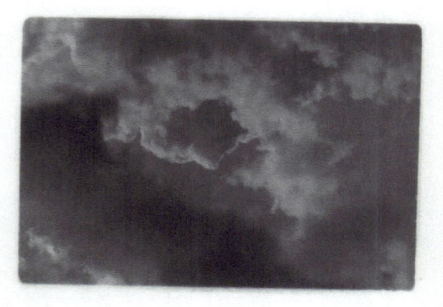

```
white, little, puffy clouds
   pinches of nothingness -
         leading

                        nowhere...
factories trying to get ahead
         in the world
   forcing thick, gray smoke

                    up

               up

       up

            to reach the sky

little innocent nothings
                    being
                            weighted

                                    down
         and choked until they

            vanish

     into the fresh air,

       leaving a dull, black shadow

         for man to cower under.
```

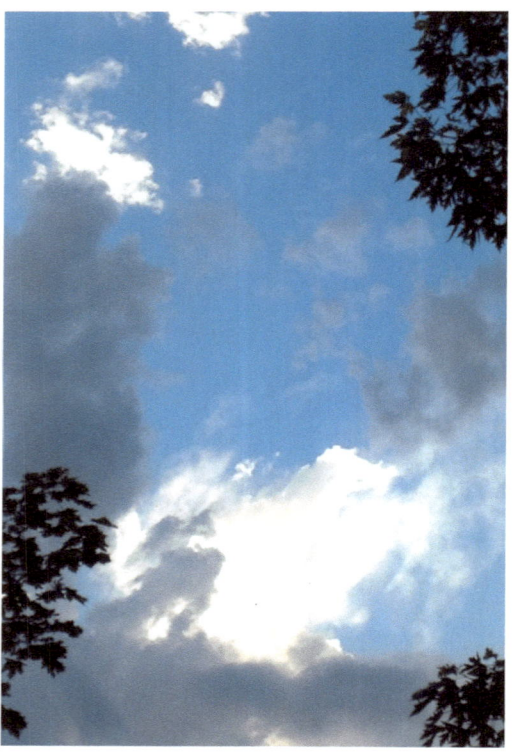

white, little puffy clouds . . .

painting love pictures in the air!
they're everywhere - but I can't
seem to mend the tears

   climate change is very real
BIG BUSINESS continues to lie

                   and steal.

e e cummings has long ago died

now I write poems that try to rhyme

there's a heaviness that sits upon
    my heart

I wonder if I can play my part

the world is cold-no, warmer now

    the clouds turn gray,

   unleash their power
d r
  o p p
    i n
      g
gentle rain in a summer shower.

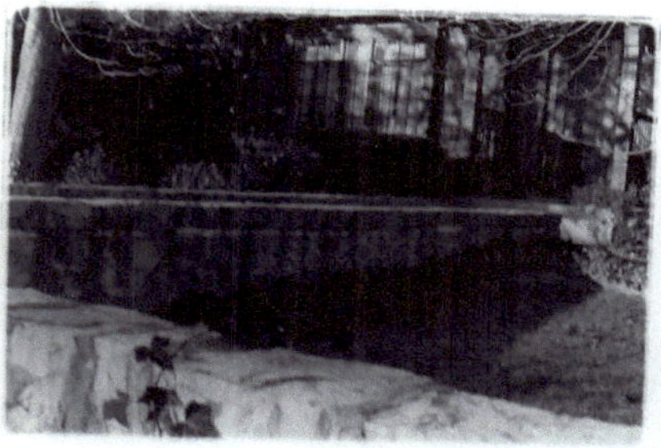

Behind Shadows of the Library Window

somewhere, outstretched
in the gloomy distance
      of the cloudless
  cloudy sky,

you sit, looking out your
   gray window,

thinking, as I am,

  of the distance between us:

of the lonliness in clouds,

and the beauty of

      an autumn day

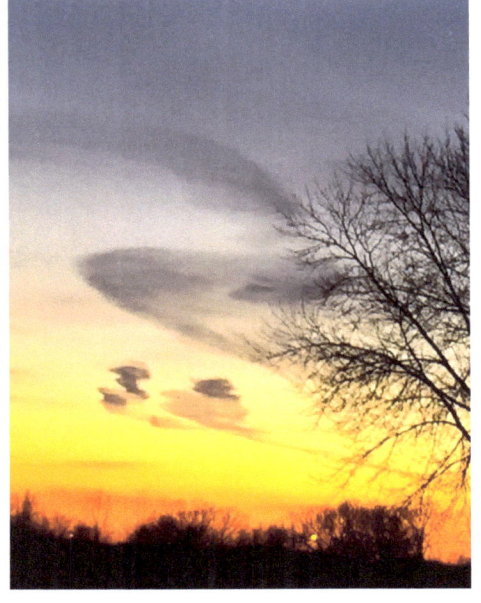

In a Lonely Tree

After many months
of searching,

she found her heart
clung tightly
to an otherwise
naked tree branch.

Hints of red passion
still evident
in the fading sun,

she could still hear
his voice

whisper her name in the wind.

peek out among the shadows
   play in the light
    dance with your slender form
the walls will not listen,

    only echo

      ...echo

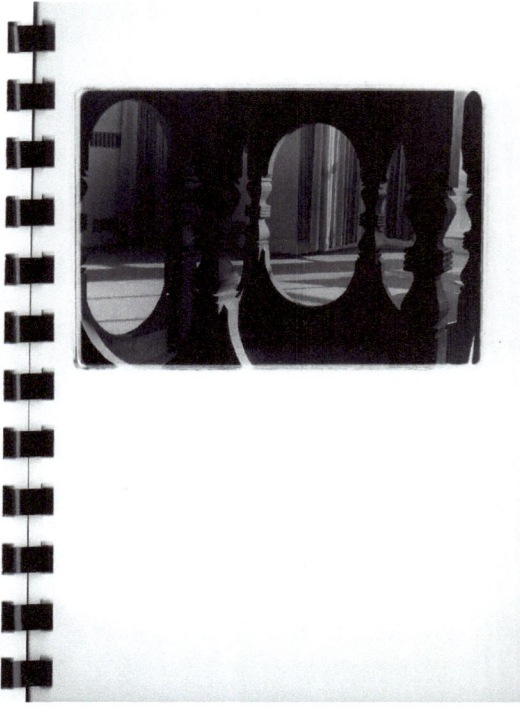

They will dance
together

In and out
of the shadows

Until the wind
carries them away

Or snow
silences
the music of the
dance.

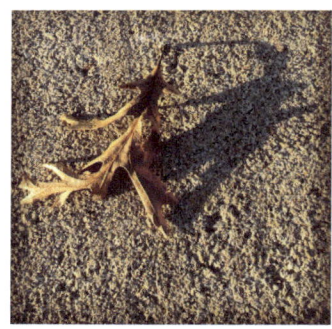

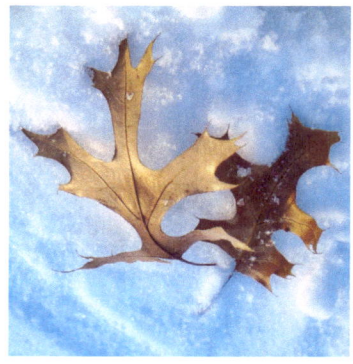

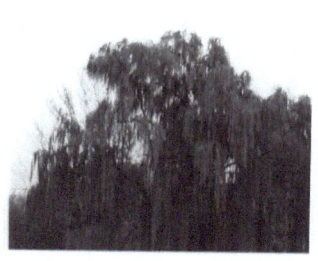

Sojourn at Dusk

So, you can see why I never ventured
   further than my willow tree

for I found contentment there –

   among the swaying branches and
      the evening air
   and the fragrant scents of
   surrounding rose bushes

      and your company

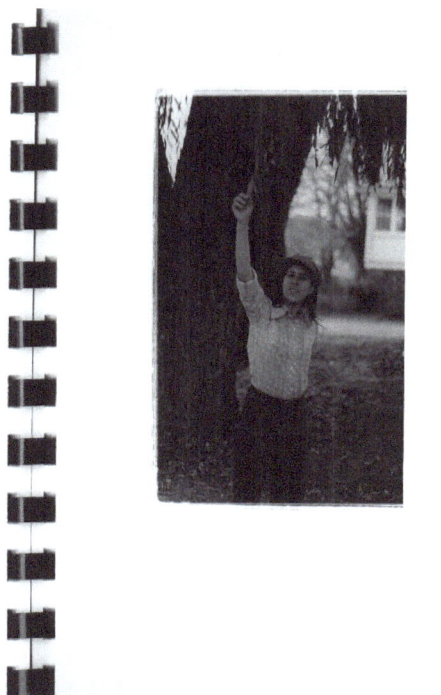

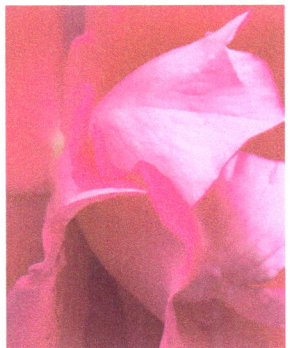

Dewdrops of Softness

In the softness of flower petals
I remember your touch
So I photograph them often,
use them as a crutch
to feel you near me when
the distance between us,
unspoken, becomes far too much.
These tears aren't for all that
might have been,
But for what we *did* have
Those two hours of eternity in the
garden.

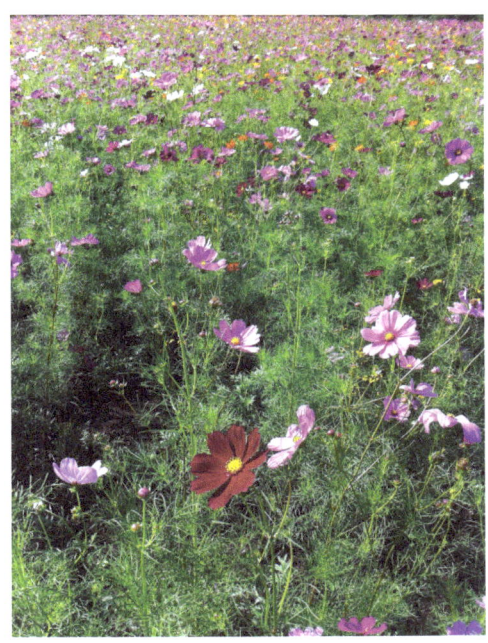

Inspiration Point

when it's dark outside
in the distant time

between morning and night

shadows of our past
cast lights

while time creates images
forgotten by an open window

The Same Moon

When I look to the sky
and notice the time

Whether morning, or night
or I manage to rhyme

Your heart beats for mine
Though I may be out of sight

A full moon shines just as bright
Despite living all these years
In two different time zones.

```
taking me back
making me remember,
is this light,
reflecting from my window

you can not see
what I find in the shadows
for it is reflections on myself
not light through open windows.
```

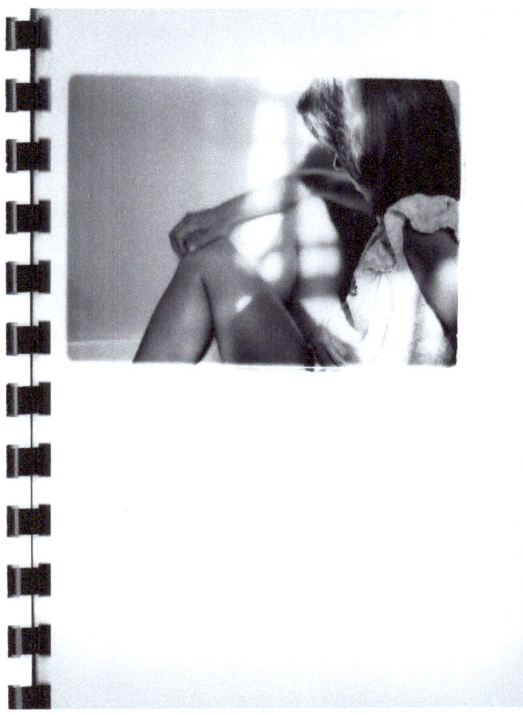

A shadow of my former self -

It's still me,
peering in the window of my soul

Pieces of me scattered,
no longer whole

Ever thinking,

Love rocks in my pockets
sinking

ever deeper into my
romantic fantasies.

Reflections of the past
cast everlasting light

slowly revealed
like light that peeks through open windows.

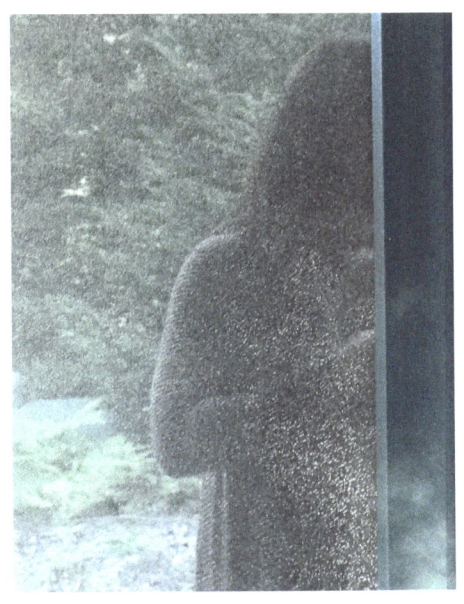